The Night Before Christmas

The Night Before Christmas

A Visit from St. Nicholas

By Clement C. Moore ❄ Illustrations by Tom Browning

STERLING CHILDREN'S BOOKS
New York

Born in Ontario, Oregon, in 1949, **Tom Browning** is an award-winning artist who has received national acclaim for both his Santa images and his fine art. Tom is the illustrator of the successful children's books, *Santa's Time Off* and *Love Me Tender*. His work is represented by the Wilcox Gallery in Jackson Hole, Wyoming.

Visit Tom online at www.tombrowning.com.

STERLING CHILDREN'S BOOKS
New York

An Imprint of Sterling Publishing
387 Park Avenue South
New York, NY 10016

STERLING CHILDREN'S BOOKS and the distinctive Sterling Children's Books logo
are registered trademarks of Sterling Publishing Co., Inc.

ISBN 978-1-4027-9004-1

Distributed in Canada by Sterling Publishing
c/o Canadian Manda Group, 165 Dufferin Street
Toronto, Ontario, Canada M6K 3H6
Distributed in the United Kingdom by GMC Distribution Services
Castle Place, 166 High Street, Lewes, East Sussex, England BN7 1XU
Distributed in Australia by Capricorn Link (Australia) Pty. Ltd.
P.O. Box 704, Windsor, NSW 2756, Australia

For information about custom editions, special sales, and premium and corporate purchases, please contact Sterling Special Sales at 800-805-5489 or specialsales@sterlingpublishing.com.

Printed in China

Lot #:
2 4 6 8 10 9 7 5 3 1
07/11

Introduction

Amid the many Christmas Eve traditions, held in various places by different persons, there was one in New York City not like any other anywhere. A company of men, women, and children would gather together just after the evening service in their church, stand around the tomb of Dr. Clement C. Moore, the author of "A Visit from St. Nicholas," and recite together the words of the poem which we all know so well and love so dearly.

Dr. Moore was born in a house near Chelsea Square, New York City, in 1781, and he lived there all his life. It was a great big house with fireplaces in it—just the house to be living in on Christmas Eve.

Dr. Moore had children. He liked writing poetry and wrote a whole book of poems for them. One year he wrote this poem, which we usually call "'Twas the Night before Christmas," to give to his children as a Christmas present. They read it just after they had hung up their stockings over one of the big fireplaces in their house. Afterward, they learned it and sometimes recited it, just as other children learn it and recite it now.

It was printed in a newspaper, then a magazine printed it, and after a time it was printed in the school readers. Later it was printed by itself, with pictures. Then it was translated into German, French, and many other languages. It was even made into "Braille," which is the raised printing that blind children read with their fingers. So it has happened that almost all the children in the world have read this poem!

Twas the night before Christmas,

When all through the house

Not a creature was stirring,

Not even a mouse;

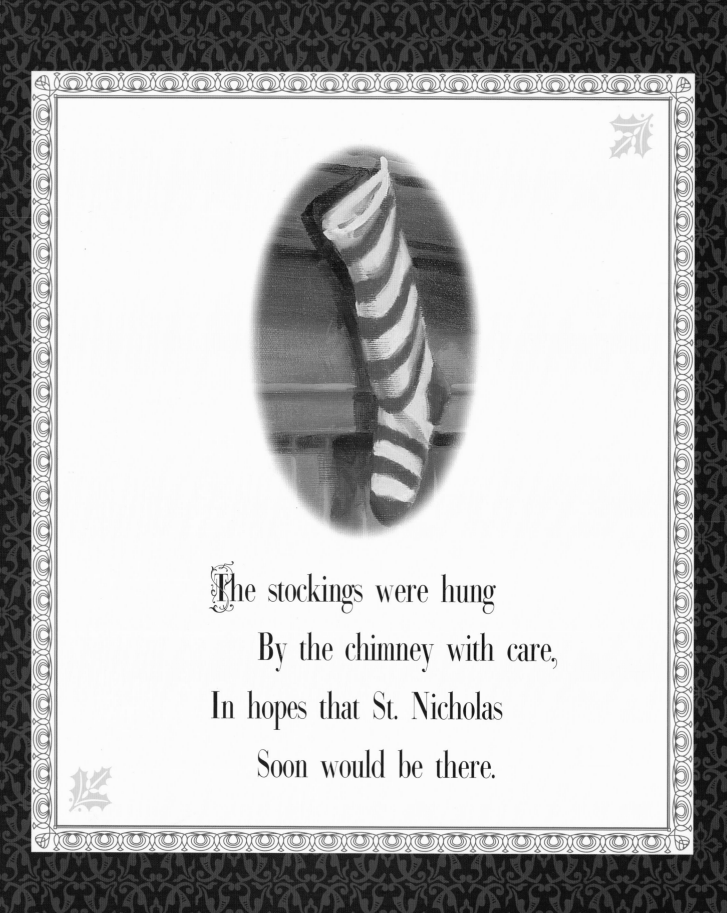

The stockings were hung
By the chimney with care,
In hopes that St. Nicholas
Soon would be there.

The children were nestled
All snug in their beds,
While visions of sugarplums
Danced in their heads;

And Mamma in her kerchief,

And I in my cap,

Had just settled our brains

For a long winter's nap,

When out on the lawn

    There arose such a clatter,

I sprang from the bed

    To see what was the matter.

Away to the window
I flew like a flash,
Tore open the shutters
And threw up the sash.

The moon on the breast
     Of the new fallen snow
Gave the luster of midday
     To objects below,

When, what to my wondering eyes
     Should appear,
But a miniature sleigh,
     And eight tiny reindeer,

With a little old driver,

So lively and quick,

I knew in a moment

It must be St. Nick.

More rapid than eagles
His coursers they came,
And he whistled, and shouted,
And called them by name,

"Now, Dasher! Now, Dancer!

Now, Prancer and Vixen!

On, Comet! On, Cupid!

On, Donder and Blitzen!

To the top of the porch!
To the top of the wall!
Now dash away! Dash away!
Dash away all!"

As dry leaves that before

The wild hurricane fly,

When they meet with an obstacle,

Mount to the sky;

So up to the housetop
The coursers they flew,
With the sleigh full of toys,
And St. Nicholas too.

And then in a twinkling,

I heard on the roof

The prancing and pawing

Of each little hoof.

As I drew in my head
And was turning around,
Down the chimney St. Nicholas
Came with a bound.

He was dressed all in fur,

From his head to his foot,

And his clothes were all tarnished

With ashes and soot;

A bundle of toys
    He had flung on his back,
And he looked like a peddler
    Just opening his pack.

His eyes, how they twinkled!
His dimples, how merry!
His cheeks were like roses,
His nose like a cherry!

His droll little mouth

Was drawn up like a bow,

And the beard of his chin

Was as white as the snow!

The stump of a pipe

He held tight in his teeth,

And the smoke, it encircled

His head like a wreath.

He had a broad face
And a little round belly,
That shook when he laughed,
Like a bowlful of jelly.

He was chubby and plump,

A right jolly old elf,

And I laughed when I saw him,

In spite of myself.

A wink of his eye

And a twist of his head,

Soon gave me to know

I had nothing to dread.

He spoke not a word,

But went straight to his work,

And filled all the stockings,

Then turned with a jerk,

And laying his finger

Aside of his nose,

And giving a nod,

Up the chimney he rose.

He sprang to his sleigh,
    To his team gave a whistle,
And away they all flew,
    Like the down of a thistle.

But I heard him exclaim,

As he drove out of sight,

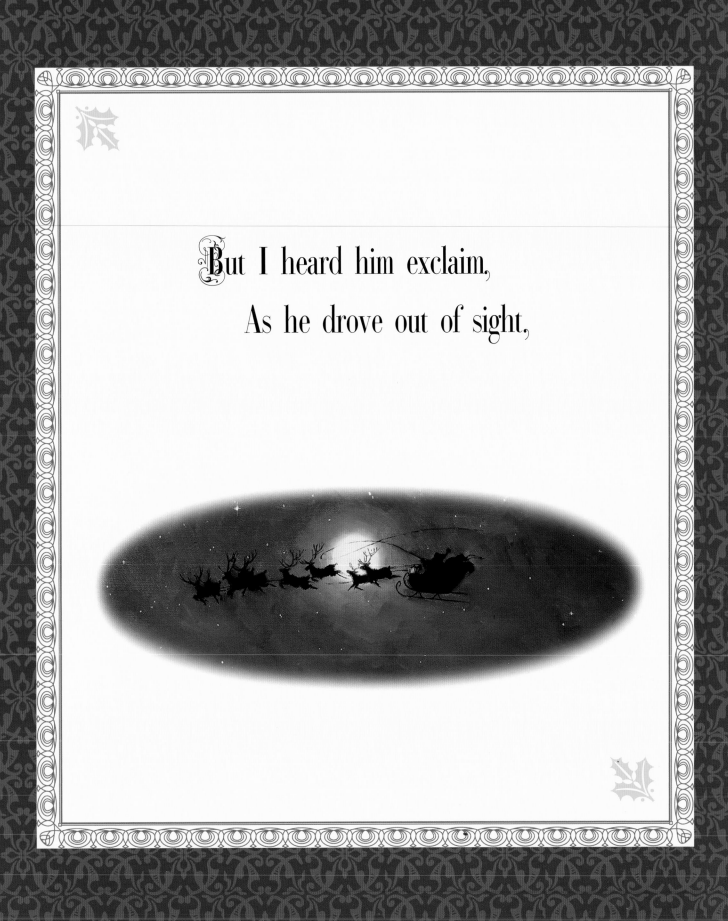

Merry Christmas to all,

And to all a good night!"

The End